Bead Loom Patterns

Easy Bead Loom Patterns & Bracelet Ideas

DEDICATION

Contents

Bead Loom Bracelets

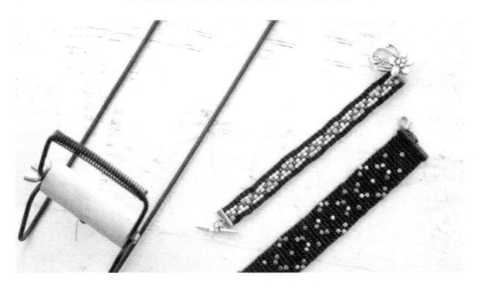

Supplies

Bead Loom Bracelet Patterns (Instructions to download are at the bottom of this post.)

Bead Loom

Beading Needle (came with loom)

Thread

Glue

Slider Clasps

Bead Loom Patterns

Jump Rings and Lobster Clasps

Size 8 Round and 3mm Cube Seed Beads (Colors and amount needed are listed on each pattern.)

Copper Metal Cube

Opaque Frosted Jet Cube

Opaque Turquoise Cube

Opaque Jet Round

Opaque Frosted White Round

Frosted Bronze Round

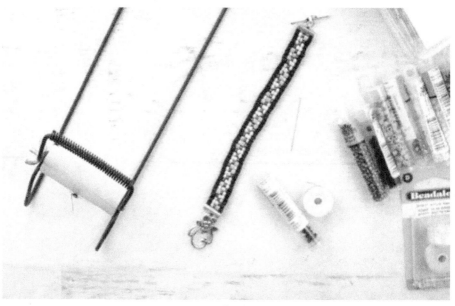

How to Make Bead Loom Bracelets

First, tie your thread in a double knot to one nail on the loom.

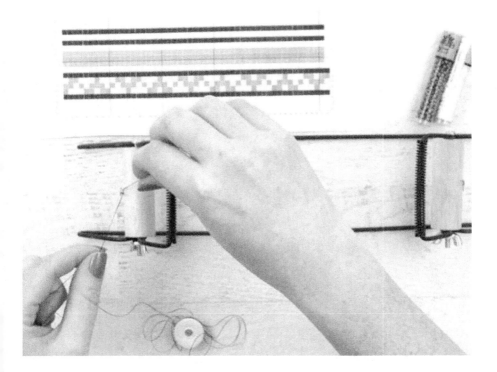

Gently stretch the thread across the loom, putting in a groove on each side as you go. Wrap the thread around the other side of the loom one time.

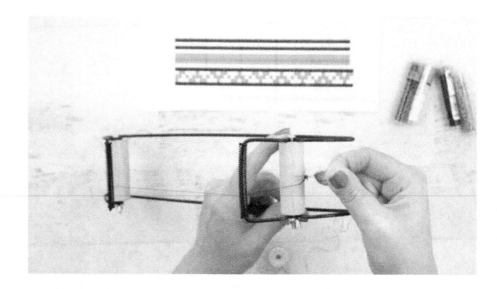

Bring the thread back across the loom, putting it through the groove next in line on each side, and wrap it around the first nail. Continue until you have one more thread than row of beads in your pattern. (For example, if you have a pattern that is 5 beads across, string 6 rows of thread.) Tie the thread off on the nail you stopped at and cut a tail a few inches long. Make sure the strings are tight. You can unscrew the dowels to loosen them and turn slightly to make it tighter.

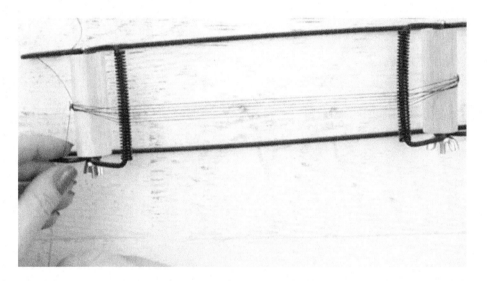

Cut a piece of thread about the size from your fingers to your shoulder and tie it onto the first strand that is going across the loom. Leave a tail about a few inches long and slide the knot as close to one side as you can. Thread the needle on the other end of the thread.

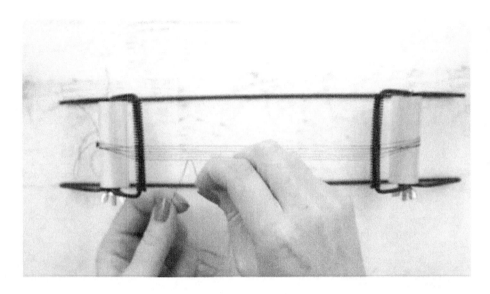

Start on one end of the pattern and string the beads on. Bring the thread and beads UNDER the thread across the loom, to the opposite side of where you tied it on.

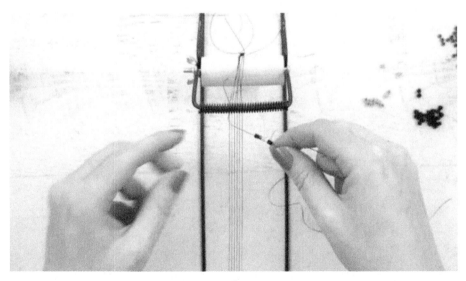

Push the beads up through the spaces between the threads on the loom.

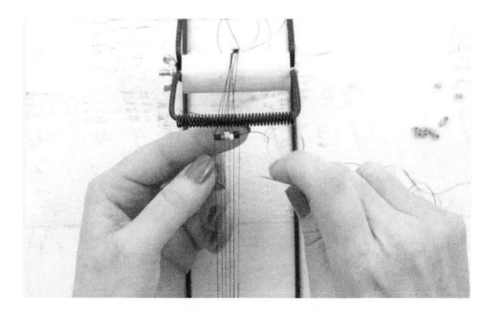

Turn the needle around and push it back through the beads, making sure it goes over the thread. Hard to explain, but definitely watch the video.

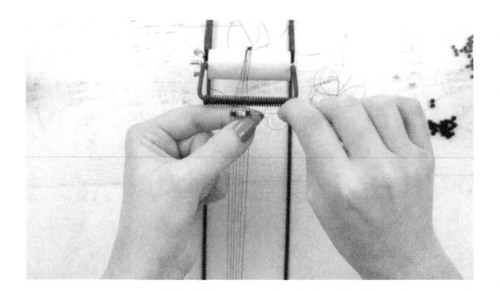

If you run out of thread before you're done, weave the excess back and forth between previous rows until it feels secure. Bring the needle back up between one of the rows and snip off the excess. Do the opposite to start a new thread. Again, the video will make much more sense.

When the bracelet is long enough, carefully cut it off the loom, keeping the strings as long as possible. Tie all of the strings together in double knots to secure the beads on the ends.

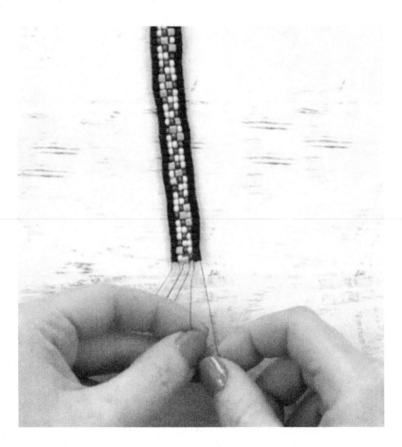

Put some strong glue on all of the knots to secure them. Let the glue dry, and then cut off the excess thread. Be careful not to cut through the knots.

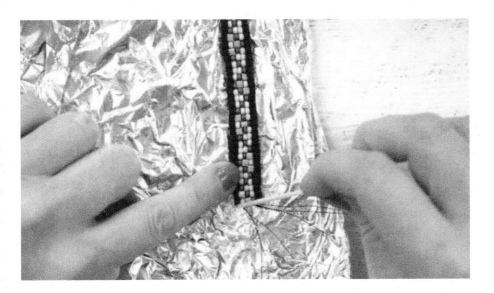

Smear a little glue on the inside of the slider clasp and slide it onto the bracelet. Close the ends.

Add a couple jump rings and a lobster clasp, and you're done! You can add more jump rings to make them bigger or even a chain to make it adjustable.

Aren't they pretty?

Beginner Loom Bracelet

Supplies

Bead Loom

220 Inches or 560cm Thread/Strand of Floss

Variety of Size 10 Seed Beads

Beading Needles

Ruler/Tape Measure

Scissors

Instructions:

Setting Up the Loom

Firstly, before you set up your loom with thread, decide how wide you want your bracelet to be. Once you've decided you'll need one strand of thread for every bead plus one.

Measure your strands of yarn that they are all 22 inches (56cm) long. Then you'll want to gather one end of the threads together and tie them in a basic knot about one inch (2.5cm) from the end. Trim the ends if necessary to make them neat.

If your loom has a tall end start by wrapping the threads around the stem of the lock several times. Then taking your threads pull them up and over the top bar of your loom. Then turn your loom around so that you can pull the threads towards you while arranging them evenly on the groves.

{Note: Do not worry if the threads aren't perfectly placed in the middle. This won't affect the outcome.}

Pull the threads down and over the bottom end, making sure to space your threads out evenly once again. NONE of the threads should cross over each other. Then wrap the remaining thread around the stems lock.

Starting Off the Bracelet

Start off by threading your needle with about 80 inches (204cm). Taking the end f your thread, tie it onto the top left-most warped thread leaving about a 2 inch (6cm) tail.

Thread 9 beads onto your needle and beading thread, then pull the beads under the warped threads, push them up between the warped threads and weave your needle back through them making sure to guide the needle OVER the warped threads.

When your bracelet is long enough, unwind it at the bottom of the loom and take it off of the loom.

Start with one end of your bracelet, then thread an outside warp/thread onto your needle and weave it into your bracelet. Weave all but the 2 center warp threads into your bracelet. You'll be usng these to create fasteners.

Thread both center threads onto your needle. Then thread 2-3 seed beads onto your needle, followed by a large round bead, and then 1 more seed bead. Push your needle back through ONLY the round bead and 2-3 seed beads. Then weave remaining thread in 2 inches (5cm). Cut off any excess thread.

Now go to the other end, and repeat Step 1 and Step 2 of Side One.

Thread both your center threads onto your needle. Thread between

15-20 seed beads onto your thread. Push your needle through the first bead, and pull tight. Before weaving in the threads into your bracelet, check if the seed bead loop isn't to big or to small for your bead on Side One. It should be just big enough to slip over the bead easily. Add or remove beads until you get the right size.

Weave the remaining thread in 2 inches (5cm). Cut off any excess thread.

Miyuki Bead Loom Cuff Bracelet

Supplies

Bead loom – mine is metallic but you have also some nice wood ones

Beading thread – Sono or Miyuki brands are great

A fine beading needle

Some miyuki delica 11/0 beads as described in the pattern

Some jewellery glue like E6000 or Hasulith

A cuff bracelet 15mm wide in gold colour with curved edges in this example which is pretty easy to do but there are also many other ways to mount your bracelet

Or if you prefer it in silver colour

DIY steps:

1. Prepare your bead loom

To prepare your bead loom, you may be able to do the full length of the bracelet if you have an adjustable loom. In that case make sure you have at least the length of the bracelet +2 cm on both sides between your 2 coils.

Then, fix your thread with a small knot on the center screw located on the wooden barrel on one side of your bead loom. From this anchor point, pull your thread through the coil on the same side a little bit offset from the center. Then cross to the other side coil, go through it and make a loop around the center screw on that side.

Go through the coil, leaving one spacer between this thread and the previous one and going towards the center, cross again to the other side, leave on spacer between this thread and the previous one, and make a loop around the screw and so on until you have 8 threads crossing the loom. It is really easy to do, believe me, even though the explanations look complicated…

Before starting, use the screws maintaining the barrels to tension the threads by rolling the barrels. It doesn't need to be super tight, but the threads should be well maintained in position to keep a regular beadwork.

2. Thread your beads row after row

Print your pattern if it is not done already.

Prepare 2m of thread and just make a simple knot on the first thread about 5 cm from the coil. Thread your needle and go through the threads installed on the loom in one direction, then come back alternatively going above and below the threads.

Do that 2 times more and you are ready to start.

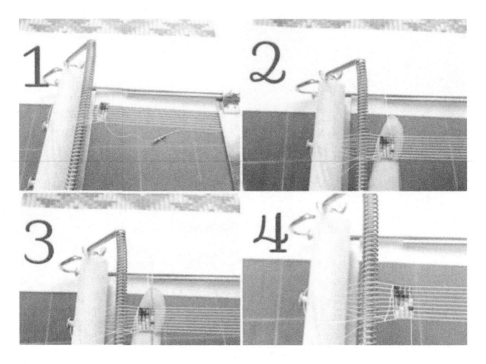

Thread your beads as per the pattern's first row.

Pass your needle below the threads. (1)

Then use your fingers to position the beads between each thread by maintaining them from below (2).

Once they are all in position, thread all the beads of this row. Your needle should go above the loom threads (3). Your row is fixed (4).

Then repeat this principle for all the rows of your beadwork. See how easy it is!

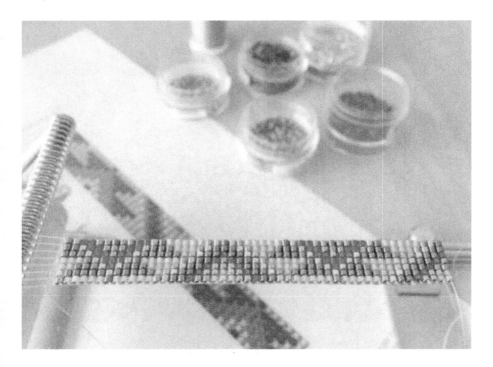

3. Renew / Hide your thread

During the beadwork, you may not have enough thread to finish. In that case, simply weave your thread back through the rows. Take a new thread, start about 5 rows before the row you stopped and weave through the rows until you reach it again. You can continue your beadwork.

If you are at the end of your beadwork, simply weave your thread back through the previous rows to hide the end thread.

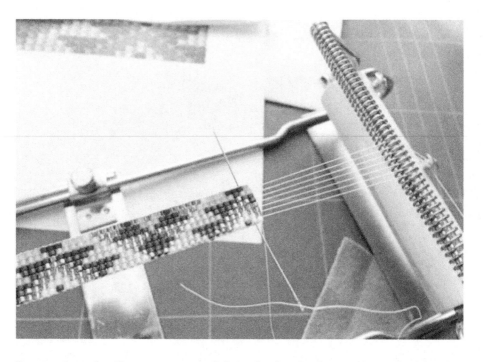

Remember the few rows you did at the beginning only with threads? Carefully remove the knot, thread your needle and weave through the first rows to hide the thread.

4. Release your beadwork from the loom

How to release your beadwork from the loom?

Warning: this part can be a bit boring. Indeed, there is not only fun in making beautiful jewellery, there are also things you need to do so that your work does not fall into pieces after a while... The principle is to cut your threads as close as possible to the screws.

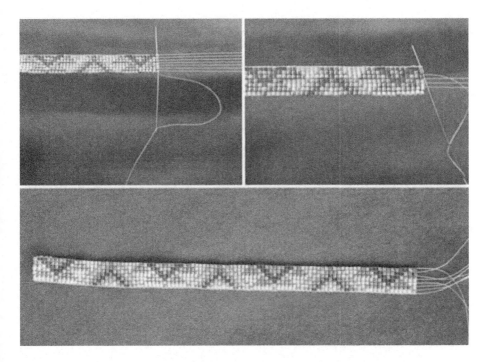

Then thread your needle with one thread and weave through the work. You have to do that with all of the threads to hide them and ensure your ends will not fray in the future.

5. Mount your beadwork on the cuff bracelet

Your weaving work is done. One more thing before mounting it on the cuff bracelet: make sure you have the correct number of rows and that it fits perfectly within the allowable space!

So once you checked that, you can use your magic glue to mount the weaving on the bracelet.

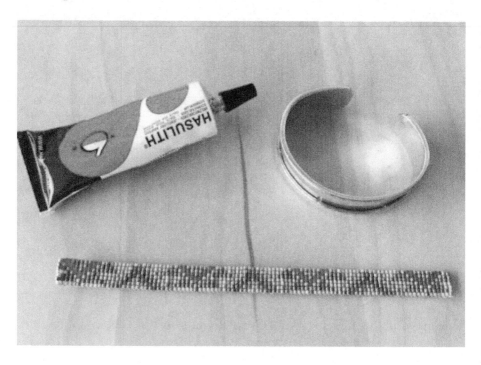

Start by one end and apply some glue.

Don't put too much or it will overflow and it is never nice.

Leave it to dry for a good 24 hours before wearing it.

And you have done a wonderful bracelet with bead looming technique.

Simple and Colorful Seed Bead Loom Bracelets

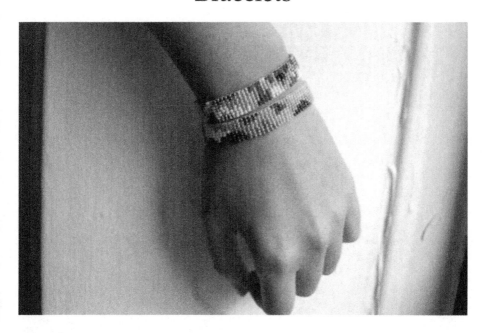

Supplies

a small box (a tissue box works really well)

a craft knife

a ruler

thread

a beading needle or beading wire

seed beads

First remove the plastic. Then, using the hole as your guide, remove the top of the box along the longer sides, leaving behind the top along the shorter sides.

Snip the sides of the remaining box top.

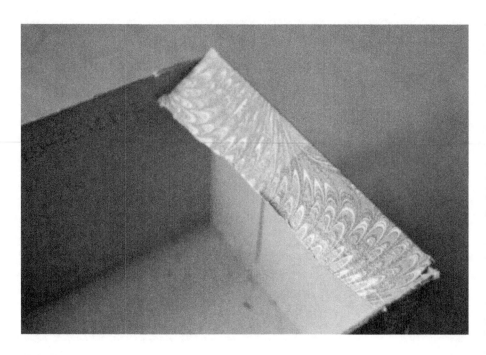

Fold down.

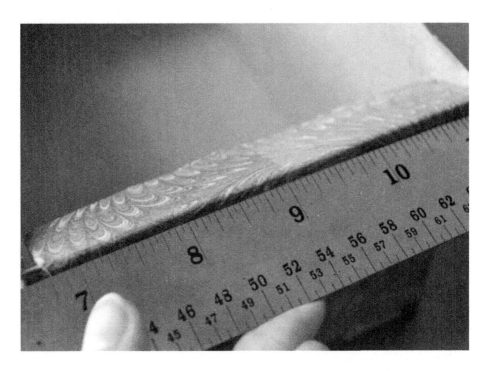

Using a ruler, cut slits along the edge, every 1/16 of an inch.

Repeat on the other side.

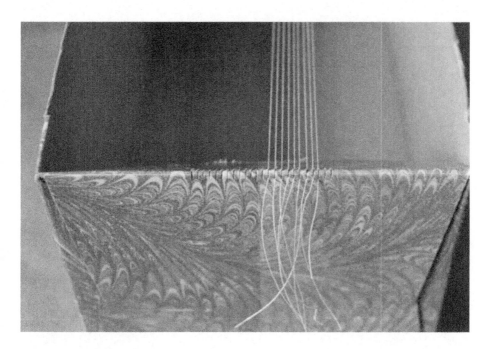

You have your loom!

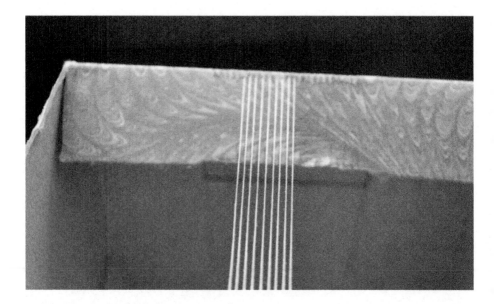

Onto bracelet making:

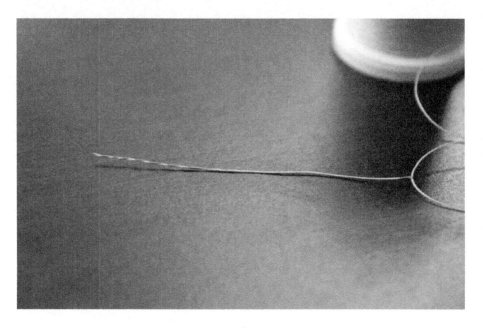

Get out your beading needle (a very thin needle) or make one using a piece of beading wire (very thin wire) folded in half and twisted at the end.

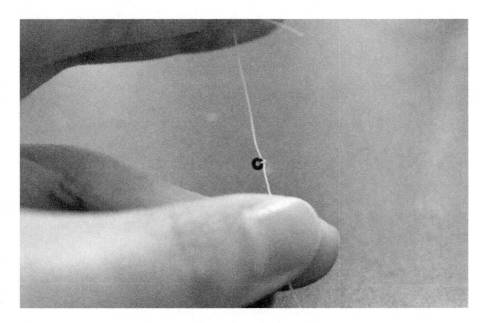

Take a long piece of thread (2-3 feet depending on how long/wide you want your bracelet) and tie a bead close to one end. This will be your stop bead, it will hold your thread in place.

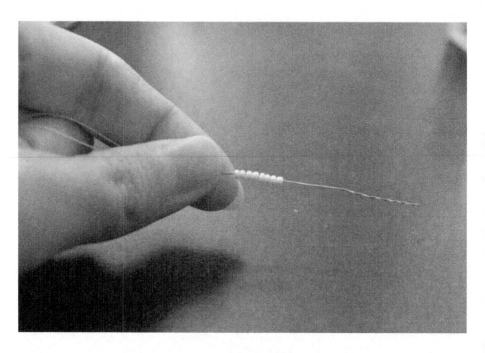

Put the same number of beads on your thread as there are spaces on your loom.

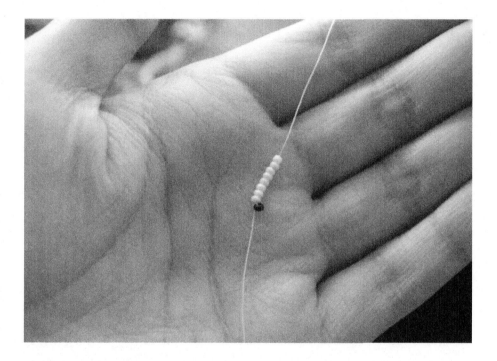

Holding the beads underneath the loom threads, pop each bead into a space and hold them there.

Then, go back through the beads OVER the threads. Be careful not to go through your stop bead.

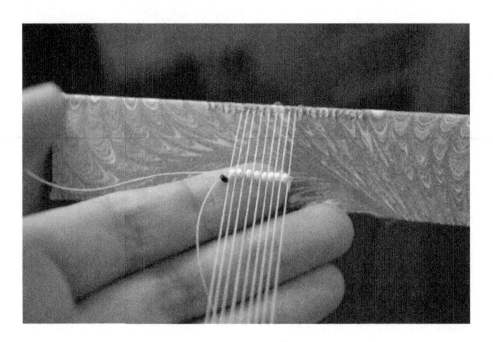

Pull it taught and repeat...

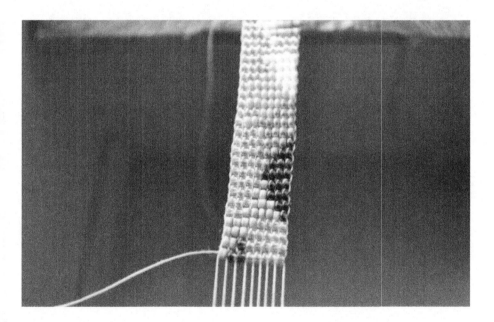

...like a lot of times.

Remove your stop bead and tie off the ends. Done! These bracelets take about the same amount of time as woven friendship bracelets but have the added advantage of not needing a pattern.

Morse Code DIY Beaded Loom Bracelet

Supplies

beading loom

Toho Round Seed Beads 11/0 Teal and Toho Round Seed Beads 11/0 Silver

Beadalon Big Eye Needles

Beadalon Wildfire thread

Stretch Magic Clear Bead Cord

Toho Round Seed Beads 8/0 Silver

QuickTite Super Glue Gel

a silver button

Design

The "dreamer" Morse Code pattern is included in the attached pdf. You can use it and skip over this step if you like. Otherwise, follow these instructions to create a bracelet with your own phrase.

Thread your beading loom according to your manufacturer's instructions. Check your gauge by beading a one inch length of bracelet. Count the beads from end to end within your inch and write down this number.

Determine the final length of your bracelet. (Subtract 1/2" if using a button closure.) Hint: Women's bracelets are typically 7" around. Men's bracelets are typically 8" around.

Multiply the number of beads per inch you counted in step 1 by the length of the bracelet you selected in step 2. This is the total number of beads of a single row of your bracelet. Write down this number.

Determine the word or phrase you want to use in your bracelet and map out the number of rows required for your finished piece. That's 2 blank rows at the top, a row for dreamer, a blank row, a row for dabbler, a blank row, a row for noodler, and 2 blank rows at the bottom.

Translate your words or phrase using a Morse Code Translator.

Copy and paste the morse code into a word processing program and enlarge the font size to make it easier to read. Count the total number of beads from end to end. Count 1 bead per dot, 2 beads per dash, 1 bead per space separating dashes and dots, 3 beads per space between letters, and 5 beads per space between words. Write down this number.

Subtract the number of beads in your word you counted in step 6 from the total number of beads in a row you calculated in step 3. This number represents the total number of extra beads you need around your word beads. Divide the extra bead number by 2 to determine the number of extra beads needed on each side of your word beads. Round to the nearest whole number (one up and one down) if necessary.

Repeat these steps for each of your words.

Transfer your design to graph paper.

Step 3: Beading

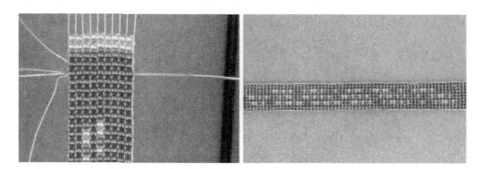

Thread your beading needle with a 2' length of beading thread.

Pick up 9 teal beads with your needle and position the needle beneath the warp threads, ensuring each bead sits between two warp threads. Hold the beads in place with your finger and gently pull the bead thread through leaving a 3" tail remaining.

Pass the needle back through the beads over the top of the warp threads. You want to pull the thread until it's taut, but you don't want to pull it too tight.

Repeat these steps following your pattern.

To change thread, leave a 3" tail of old thread, and a 3" tail of new thread. These will be worked into the piece later.

Step 4: Finishing

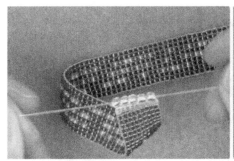 

Use your needle to weave the thread tails back into the beads.

Cut the warp threads and weave the tails back into the beads.

To each end of the bracelet, run a length of thread through the last row of beads and add five larger seed beads. Secure each bead in place and weave in the thread tails.

On one end, add stretchable clear bead cord through the large beads. Thread on six or seven more large beads to create a loop long enough to go around your button.

Tie off the cord with an overhand knot and add a drop of quick drying glue to lock in place.

On the other end, run a length of thread through the row of large beads and add your button. Secure the button in place and weave in the thread tails.

Coachella Inspired Beaded Bracelet

Supplies

FCO-9093 - Miyuki Findings Gold Plated 2 Loop Seed Bead Slide End
Tubes 35mm (2)

Project uses 1 Set. You will need 1 package.

FCL-3049 - 22K Gold Plated Toggle Clasps 9mm (5 Sets)

Project uses 2 Sets. You will need 1 package.

FJR-3914 - 22K Gold Plated Open Jump Rings 4mm 20 Gauge 22k Gold Plated (100)

Project uses 12 pieces. You will need 1 package.

DB-351 - Miyuki Delica Seed Beads 11/0 Matte White DB351 7.2 Grams

Project uses 1 Tube. You will need 1 package.

DB-753 - Miyuki Delica Seed Beads 11/0 Opaque Matte Red DB753 7.2 Grams

Project uses 1 Tube. You will need 1 package.

DB-310 - Miyuki Delica Seed Beads 11/0 'Matte Black Opaque' DB310 7.2 Grams

Project uses 1 Tube. You will need 1 package.

DB-1583 - Miyuki Delica Seed Beads 11/0 Matte Opaque Mandarin Orange DB1583 7.2 GR

Project uses 1 Tube. You will need 1 package.

DB-1586 - Miyuki Delica Seed Beads 11/0 - Matte Opaque Sea Opal - DB1586 (8 Grams)

Project uses 1 Tube. You will need 1 package.

DB-1582 - Miyuki Delica Seed Beads 11/0 Matte Opaque Canary Yellow DB1582 7.2 Grams

Project uses 1 Tube. You will need 1 package.

DB-1588 - Miyuki Delica Seed Beads 11/0 Matte Opaque Cyan Blue DB1588 7.2 Grams

Project uses 1 Tube. You will need 1 package.

XCR-8901 - NYMO Nylon Beading Thread Size D for Delica Beads White 64YD (58 Meters)

Project uses 1 Spool. You will need 1 package.

RECOMMENDED TOOLS:

XTL-5700 - Fiskars 5 Precision Tip Scissors - Super Sharp

XTL-5511 - Beadsmith Jeweller's Micro Pliers Chain Nose Flat Nose

XTL-5514 - Beadsmith Jewelry Fine Round Nose Micro Pliers

XTL-6117 - BeadSmith Ricks Beading Loom Kit For Beginners - Weave Necklaces Bracelets And More!

XTL-3021 - Tulip Loom Work Beading Needles 90x0.5mm - 3 Pack

XTL-0106 - BeadSmith Cordless Thread Zap II Thread Burner Tool

Use white NYMO thread to set up your beading loom with 28 warp threads about 5 1/4 inches long. Remember, this is the length from the outside edges of the warp rods.

As demonstrated in the video, begin to weave your bracelet. Using size 11/0 Miyuki Delica beads. Follow the pattern provided.

Finish the piece as shown in the video, removing it from the loom, spreading the beads evenly to take up the slack in the warp threads, and then tie off and weave in your thread tails.

Use pliers to fold down one end on a gold plated 2 loop tube slide end. Slide the last row of your woven piece into the tube, and then bend down the other end of the tube. Repeat with the second tube slide end on the other end of your woven piece.

To one end, open one jump ring and attach it to the loop of one slide end. Close the jump ring. Add three more jump rings. To the final jump ring, attach one bar from the toggle clasp set. Repeat for the other side of this slide end.

To the other end, open one jump ring and attach it to the loop of one slide end. Close the jump ring. Add one more jump ring. To that final jump ring, attach one circle from the toggle clasp set. Repeat for the other side of this slide end.

All done!

Printed in Great Britain
by Amazon

46406415R00036